GOD'S PLAN

for Growing the Christian Church

CHUCK BROWN

WESTBOW
PRESS®
A DIVISION OF THOMAS NELSON
& ZONDERVAN

WestBow Press books may be ordered through booksellers or by contacting:

WestBow Press
A Division of Thomas Nelson & Zondervan
1663 Liberty Drive
Bloomington, IN 47403
www.westbowpress.com
844-714-3454

ISBN: 978-1-6642-2069-0 (sc)
ISBN: 978-1-6642-2070-6 (hc)
ISBN: 978-1-6642-2068-3 (e)

Library of Congress Control Number: 2021901378

Print information available on the last page.

WestBow Press rev. date: 07/10/2023

Contents

Preface

What is God's plan? It is the principles that Jesus taught in the Bible. This book teaches these principles in a systematic way so that it is easier to see the plan and obey it. This book is based upon the Gospels: Matthew, Mark, Luke, and John. I limited the book to these Gospels because I believe that, in them, Jesus taught all that was needed to establish and grow the Christian Church.

I began writing this book without having any preconceived idea of the plan. My mind was a blank slate to begin with. When I read the Scriptures, my mind automatically categorized them into ideas or patterns of thought, which helped me see the big picture systematically. I placed these Scriptures into categories that helped me analyze them until I could see a unifying pattern. In the case of this book, I called this pattern *God's Plan for Growing the Christian Church.*

I began with a three-ring binder that had separators for each category I had found, and I began placing Scriptures into these categories until I found an outline of the plan; then, for each category item, I made sure that the Scriptures related to that category. In deciding which Scriptures to include in the book, I let the preponderance of the evidence decide that. If there were multiple Scriptures that said the same thing, I selected the one that said it best. When deciding when to use a Scripture, I let the theme or direction of the Scriptures decide when to use them so that there was a natural fit. For each Scripture used in this book, I wrote a statement according to the way I see God's plan for God's disciples.

I renamed the 25 "categories" to 25 "chapters"; and put them into 9 groups and into sequences that helps a person to see how the 25 chapters logically fit together. I wrote a summary page for each group and wrote a short statement for each summary and each chapter of the summary group.

The last chapter of the book called Gospel Presentation is intended to be used for sharing the gospel with an unbeliever for salvation purposes or with a believer for educational purposes.

Since this book was researched, designed, and written in a systematic way, I am confident that this book shares with disciples how to obey God's plan, to live it successfully, and to duplicate the plan's process over and over again to grow the Christian Church.

Summary 1

⚜

CHRIST THROUGH GOD'S PLAN

Summary 1 chapters express the relationship Jesus has with his disciples. Christ the King and his disciples were given a mission and a plan for creating and growing the Christian Church.

Christ

Jesus Christ is the King of both the Jews and the believers. He has the authority to issue commands and teachings that have to be obeyed. The Jews did not accept or obey him as King because he did not meet their expectations of a king. Jesus's disciples accepted him as King because they believed in his teachings and miracles.

Disciples

Jesus was sent from his home in heaven to be the Father's representative here on earth. Jesus taught his disciples to be his representatives on earth too. The Father told Jesus the plan, and Jesus taught the plan to his disciples. Since Jesus was perfect, he was the personification of God's plan because he lived it. After establishing the Christian Church, Jesus left his home on earth and returned to his home in heaven.

Mission

Jesus was sent to earth with the mission of sharing the good news of the kingdom of God. His mission had three facets to it: preaching, teaching, and healing. His healing authenticated his preaching and teaching messages that he was the Messiah who was sent by God to save his people. Before he went back to heaven, Jesus gave his disciples what is called the Great Commission, which was to continue the mission of making disciples of all nations.

God's Plan

Jesus said that he is the way, the truth, and the life and the only way to the Father. What does this mean? It means that not all "roads" lead to heaven. In fact, Jesus said that narrow is the road that leads to heaven and that broad is the road that leads to hell. He did not say it was the easiest road to follow but that it was the only road to follow if you want to get to heaven.

CHRIST

❧

Jesus is the King of the Jews. He is also King of his disciples. He has the authority to issue commands and teachings that need to be obeyed.

One of the reasons the Jews did not accept Jesus as their King is that they expected the Christ to be a conquering king who would free them from Roman rule. Jesus did not come as a conquering Messiah as they expected; he came as a humble servant who taught and preached a message of repentance and faith and performed many miracles. His disciples observed the miracles and teachings and believed and accepted him as their King, someone to be followed and obeyed. They believed Jesus knew, taught, and lived God's plan for having eternal life. In the beginning, they did not understand Jesus would have to die to fulfill God's plan to make eternal life a reality (Mark 9:31-32).

The good news is that Jesus died and made eternal life a reality and he made it possible for everyone who has ever lived. There is a condition for entering eternal life: one must have put his or her faith in Jesus as Savior and Lord (John 3:16).

The Bible is clear about Jesus being the King, Christ, Messiah, and Son of God. Today's disciples should obey and follow Jesus as he taught and lived, according to God's plan.

Jesus declared to the Samaritan woman, whom he met at the well, that he was the Messiah and Christ that everyone had been waiting for. He explained God's plan to the Samaritans for entering eternal life, and many became believers (John 4:25–26; John 4:39–41).

Jesus declared to the Jewish leaders that he was the Christ, Son of man and Son of God, but they did not believe him (Luke 22:66–71).

Jesus declared to Pilate, the governor, that he was King of the Jews and his kingdom was from another world. He said he had come into the world to testify to the truth of God's plan (Luke 23:1–3; John 18:36–37).

Jesus demonstrated he was the sovereign King by using his authority and power over creation—nature, demons, sickness, and death.

An example of Jesus's authority over nature is when he commanded the waves, in a furious storm, to be still, and they obeyed him (Matthew 8:23–27).

An example of Jesus's authority over demons is when he rebuked them and cast them out. The demons obeyed his command because they knew he was the Christ and Son of God and had the authority to do so (Luke 4:41).

An example of Jesus's authority over sickness is when he touched Peter's mother-in-law who had a fever and the fever left her (Matthew 8:14–15).

An example of Jesus's authority over death is when he was able to bring a dead girl back to life (Matthew 9:23–25).

Discussion Questions

1. Why did the Jews not believe Jesus was the Christ?

2. Why did the disciples believe Jesus was the Christ?

3. In the beginning, what did the disciples not understand about Jesus?

4. What kind of relationship should believers have with Jesus?

5. What caused the Samaritans to believe Jesus was the Christ?

6. Where did Jesus say his kingdom was from?

7. How did Jesus demonstrate he had authority over all creation?

8. Why did the Jewish leaders want to take Jesus to Pilate?

DISCIPLES

◈

A disciple of Christ is any follower or pupil of Christ. To his disciples, Jesus was the rabbi or teacher who taught them God's plan. Jesus first learned God's plan from the Father (John 12:49). Then he was sent into the world to teach it to his disciples (John 17:18). Finally, he sent his disciples into the world to teach God's plan to all nations. (Matthew 28:18–20).

Jesus said he wants disciples who have counted the cost of being his disciple and are still willing to commit to following him. Following Jesus can cost a disciple his or her freedom, job, friends, family, material possessions, and even his or her life. There are things that bring pleasure to believers' lives that have nothing to do with serving Christ; Jesus wants believers to be willing to give up doing those things if they conflict with following God's plan. Jesus died on the cross because he lived according to God's plan, and he wants believers to be willing to do the same. Jesus wants disciples who are not ashamed of living according to God's plan. For those who are ashamed of Jesus and God's plan, Jesus will be ashamed of them on Judgment Day (Mark 8:34–38). Living according to God's plan should make a believer's way of living appear attractive to nonbelievers.

Believers should be so committed to God and following his plan that when they find out how to obtain eternal life, they should be willing to give up all they have and are doing to work their own plan and, instead, follow God's plan. Eternal life is worth giving up everything our temporal lives can offer because living according to one's own plans will lead to an eternity with Satan in hell, while living according to God's plan leads to an eternity with God in heaven (Matthew 13:44–46).

CHUCK BROWN

Discussion Questions

1. Who is a disciple of Christ?

2. What should disciples do when they learn that an aspect of their lives is in conflict with God's plan?

3. What will happen on Judgment Day if a disciple is ashamed of Christ and God's plan?

MISSION

❧

Every person has been created by God, and God has a mission for every person. Some accept God's grace and learn and obey the mission—these are Christians. Others never accept the grace or learn or obey the mission—these are non-Christians. This book explains what the mission is and God's plan for sharing that mission.

Jesus said his mission was to preach the good news of the kingdom of God (Luke 4:43). He preached the good news to a mostly Jewish audience, which had been looking forward to the coming of the Messiah to establish an earthly kingdom and be a conquering king who would free them from Roman rule and oppression. But that is not the kind of kingdom he came to establish, so many of the Jews did not accept him as the Messiah.

Jesus was sent by God to preach the good news of the kingdom of God. The good news is that the Messiah has come to provide salvation for his disciples so that they can experience eternal life with him. He came to establish and grow his kingdom here on earth and to teach his disciples how to follow God's plan. His disciples did not understand that he had to die for their sins, be resurrected, and ascend to heaven as a part of God's plan.

Jesus came preaching a message of repentance (Matthew 4:17). Jesus wanted people to stop thinking and behaving in a self-centered manner. He wanted people to stop living according to their own plans and to start living according to God's plan. The kingdom of God is near because the time is running out before Jesus returns in judgment. Jesus has already come; he did all that was needed to break the bondage to sin and make it possible to live in freedom with God. With the mission of the first coming accomplished, the mission of the

Second Coming is near. This is an urgent message because although salvation is a free offer, it is also a limited-time offer. People need to accept Jesus as their Savior and King before his Second Coming or before they die in their sins; otherwise, they will have an eternity in hell waiting for them as their destiny after judgment. But if they accept Jesus as their Savior and King, their eternal destiny after judgment is in heaven. There is a choice, and it must be made before you die or Jesus returns, whichever comes first.

Jesus's mission had three facets to it: preaching, teaching, and healing. He preached the urgent message that the kingdom of God was near, he taught God's plan in the synagogues, and he healed those who needed healing of various ailments. His healing authenticated his preaching and teaching messages—that he was the Messiah who was sent by God to save his people.

Jesus sent his twelve apostles with the mission of preaching the same urgent message that John the Baptist preached and that Jesus had preached earlier—that people need to repent because the kingdom of God is near. And he gave his apostles the power to heal so the people would know the apostles too had been sent by God to save the people through Jesus the Messiah.

Jesus's final mission to his apostles, called the Great Commission, was to make disciples of all nations, teaching them God's plan, which went beyond preaching and healing; it included everything Jesus had taught them, which later was written in the four Gospels: Matthew, Mark, Luke, and John (Matthew 28:19–20). This book *God's Plan* is based on what is taught in those four Gospels. I believe Jesus taught all that was needed to get the kingdom established and growing. After Jesus ascended into heaven, he sent his Holy Spirit to help his apostles spread the message with power.

Discussion Questions

1. What is the good news of the kingdom of God?

2. What does it mean to repent?

3. What did healing do for the other two facets of Jesus's mission?

4. What was the first mission that Jesus sent his twelve apostles to perform?

5. What was the final mission that Jesus sent his twelve apostles to perform?

GOD'S PLAN

In the Bible, Jesus made a promise to his disciples where he said, " My Father's house has many rooms; if that were not so, would I have told you that I am going there to prepare a place for you? ³ And if I go and prepare a place for you, I will come back and take you to be with me that you also may be where I am. (John 14:2-4) Notice that Jesus stated that he knew the way to heaven, but even better than that he also said in John 14:6, "I am the way and the truth and the life. No one comes to the Father except through me."

Thomas asked Jesus a question many disciples ask: How does a person get to the Father's house in heaven? What is the plan? The plan is to receive Jesus as Savior and to follow and obey him as Lord because he is the only way to the Father's house in heaven. Heaven is the place where disciples go to after their work on earth is done. They leave their temporary residences on earth to go to their eternal homes in heaven. If disciples want to know what to do to get there, they should study and follow Jesus as their role model. Know the words and works of Jesus and try to do the same. This book tries to teach the words and works of Jesus in a systematic way so God's plan may be more clearly seen.

Jesus said he was the light of the world. Just as the pillar of fire led the Israelites through the wilderness, Jesus led his disciples during his ministry in the world. The world is a dark place, but disciples were given Jesus, who is the light of the world, to help them see clearly the plan to heaven (John 8:12). Because Jesus obeyed God's plan perfectly, he is the personification of God's light. Disciples should get to know their Bible inside and out so they can clearly see the plan. Today, disciples have the Holy Spirit as their light to reveal God's plan to them so they can follow Jesus as Lord. The Holy Spirit reminds disciples of the words and works of Jesus that are recorded in the Bible.

People have a choice, just as Adam and Eve had a choice; they could have obeyed God or Satan. One choice leads to life and the other leads to death. One leads to light and the other to darkness. One pleases God, and the other pleases self and Satan. One satisfies the cravings of the new nature, and the other satisfies cravings of the old sin nature. People who obey God have God's help in achieving God's plan. Satan does not want people to achieve God's plan. Satan tempts everyone to do anything but God's plan. The Christian lifestyle should be such that people acknowledge that what Christians have done has been through God. Non-Christians should take notice and ask where Christians get this way of living, and Christians should be prepared to answer them. The Christian lifestyle should be attractive to non-Christians who are seeking God. Christians are to live lives of righteousness by yielding to the Holy Spirit, who works in them and through them.

The road to God's house is narrow because, as Jesus said, he was the only way to the Father. The road to Satan's house is wide because it includes any and all ways except God's way. Only a few find God's way because many are blinded by sin from seeing it (Matthew 7:13–14). Man's spiritual eyes have been blinded to the truth because of sin. The only way to overcome this sin problem is through salvation. Believers have been saved, and their eyes have been opened to be able to see the truth. Believers are to seek the spiritually blind and share God's plan with them.

Jesus said believers following God's plan would sometimes experience times of trial and tribulation, and he told the following parable about it:

> Therefore, everyone who hears these words of mine
> and puts them into practice is like a wise man who
> built his house on the rock. The rain came down, the

streams rose, and the winds blew and beat against that
house; yet it did not fall, because it had its foundation
on the rock. But everyone who hears these words of
mine and does not put them into practice is like a
foolish man who built his house on sand. The rain
came down, the streams rose, and the winds blew and
beat against that house, and it fell with a great crash.
(Matthew 7:24–27)

When times of trial and tribulation come, those who persevere in
following God's plan will stand in victory, but those who do not will
fall in defeat. Get the support of other believers to help and advise
you on how to make it through these times. Satan wants believers to
fail and give up, but God wants them to withstand the trouble and
have victory.

Come to me, all you who are weary and burdened,
and I will give you rest. Take my yoke upon you and
learn from me, for I am gentle and humble in heart,
and you will find rest for your souls. For my yoke is
easy and my burden is light. (Matthew 11:28–30)

Learn God's plan because while you are doing it, you can rest
assured that God is on your side, giving you a rest that only he can
give. This is a rest benefit that affects your entire being: physical,
mental, and spiritual.

Having a relationship with God is the only way to receive this rest,
peace, and satisfaction. Taking on God's yoke, or God's plan, brings
with it the fruit of the Holy Spirit, which is love, joy, peace, patience,
kindness, goodness, faithfulness, gentleness, and self-control. Anyone
seeking these traits, or fruits, should accept Jesus as his or her Savior
and begin to follow him as Lord by obeying God's plan.

Discussion Questions

1. Why is Jesus considered the personification of God's plan?

2. Why did Jesus say he was the light of the world?

3. Why is the narrow gate considered God's plan?

4. Why is the broad gate considered Satan's plan?

Summary 2

———— ❧ ————

SECURITY THROUGH REWARDS

Summary 2 chapters explain some of the benefits of following God's plan. In this lifetime, a couple of the benefits are financial security and exhibiting the fruit of the Holy Spirit, which are the character traits that help us to grow into the image of Jesus. After this lifetime here on earth, one of the benefits are rewards that we won't know about until we get to heaven.

Security

God wants his disciples to trust him for their temporal needs, such as food, shelter, and clothing. As a disciple follows God's plan, God promises to meet said temporal needs. God does not want his disciples to worry or to have "little faith" about whether they will have enough financial resources to last during their time here on earth. God provides financial resources on a just-in-time basis, and disciples are to be good stewards of these resources. The financial resources would come from teaching their disciples God's plan, thus following the principle that the worker is worth his keep.

Fruitfulness

God wants Christians to resemble his Son, Jesus Christ. As Christians work God's plan, God changes them so that they become more fruitful and exhibit more of the fruit of the Holy Spirit, with traits such as love, joy, peace, patience, kindness, goodness, faithfulness, gentleness, and self-control. Some people believe that they are Christians because they do good works, but being a Christian is more than that. Jesus said that Christians must first be in him by accepting Jesus as their Savior and obeying him as Lord. Some people believe they can inherit salvation because their parents are Christians, but salvation does not work that way; each person must individually accept Jesus as Savior and Lord. Then, as they obey God's plan, they will produce the fruit that God desires.

Rewards

In heaven, Jesus rewards disciples who have followed God's plan on earth. Some of these rewards are for service they have performed for fellow believers. These don't have to be large or complex deeds, just simple ones. Jesus also provides rewards for loving their enemies. God gives believers rewards for how they use his wealth. He wants believers to use his wealth for helping people, not for trying to hold on to as much as they can, to become rich, as if it is theirs; it's his. When unbelievers see or hear about these deeds, they may want to become believers too. God gives rewards for doing good deeds in private. God does not give rewards when believers receive praises and prizes from others in public since they would have already been rewarded. God will give believers rewards for enduring persecution. Some unbelievers will hate believers for their message and may try to keep them from sharing God's plan.

Prayer

A new believer should be taught about prayer. Prayer is talking with God and making your needs and wants known to him. God likes prayer because it expresses the believer's trust and dependency on God to provide those needs and wants. Prayer can be done alone or in a group.

SECURITY

God wants believers to trust him to meet their temporal needs. As believers trust and obey God's plan, he promises to provide the financial resources they need for things like food, shelter, and clothing. God does not want believers to worry about whether they are making or have accumulated enough money and material goods, for God knows their financial needs and will supply them on a just-in-time basis. The money and material goods belong to God, and he wants believers to be good stewards of these resources. Unbelievers believe the money and material goods belong to them and that they should make and accumulate as much as they can so they can retire with a feeling of financial security. Money and material goods, however, are here today and gone tomorrow and cannot be trusted to bring financial security. God is the believers' security. They are to do the work of making disciples and not worry about chasing after money. He wants disciples to put their faith for their financial security in him alone. Jesus does not want his disciples to have doubts or "little faith" in believing God will provide for them (Matthew 6:19–34; Luke 12:22–24).

Jesus tells a story of a rich man who had a big harvest and decided his barns were not big enough to contain it all. He decided to tear down his barns and build bigger ones so he could retire, take life easy, and eat, drink, and be merry. In God's kingdom, there is no retirement. Money and material wealth are not to be stored up for the purpose of resting and living in retirement. Every day God gives believers is to be used to serve him by obeying God's plan (Luke 12:16–21).

The usual way that God provided money for Jesus and his

disciples was through paying them for their teaching and preaching in the synagogues, based on the principle that "the worker is worth his keep" (Matthew 10:5–16; Luke 10:1–7).

A synagogue had somewhere near ten or more families in it. The ruling elder of the synagogue would find a traveling rabbi to teach on the Sabbath. The elder and rabbis were paid for their services by the tithe and offerings from the families they served in the synagogue.

Disciples have their security in God. As they work God's plan, God provides for their daily needs. God's provision usually comes from the people who benefit from the disciples' teaching. Disciples need not worry about their provision. As the Scripture says, "Seek first his kingdom and his righteousness, and all these things will be given to you as well" (Matthew 6:33). *"All these things"* are the daily needs for which God provides. So, by working God's plan, disciples are compensated by God, in whom they have their security.

Discussion Questions

1. To whom do money and material goods belong?

2. What is the purpose of money and material goods from the disciples' perspective?

3. What is the purpose of money and material goods from the unbelievers' perspective?

4. Financial security comes from doing what?

5. When does retirement begin?

6. Under what principle did Jesus and his disciples get paid for working God's plan?

FRUITFULNESS

❧

God wants Christians to resemble his Son Jesus Christ so as they work God's plan with the help of the Holy Spirit they grow progressively as God matures or changes them through the second step of salvation (which is called sanctification) so they can become more fruitful and exhibit more of the traits or fruit of the Holy Spirit, such as love, joy, peace, patience, kindness, goodness, faithfulness, gentleness, and self-control.

Some people believe they are Christians because they do good works, which makes them appear to be Christians. Being a Christian is more than just appearances. Christians must be in Jesus by trusting and obeying him as Lord. He said that as Christians follow God's plan, they will grow and mature in him bearing much fruit and he will give them whatever they ask in his name so they can be even more fruitful. Jesus also said that if you don't remain in him, you will not bear any fruit and will be sent to hell for all eternity (John 15:4–8).

Some people believe they are Christians because their parents are Christians, but that's not how salvation works. You cannot inherit salvation; each person must personally make a decision to accept Jesus as his or her Savior and Lord. As believers repent of their own plans and follow God's plan, they will grow in Christ and produce the fruit that God desires (Luke 3:8).

Discussion Questions

1. How are Christians to grow in the fruit of the Holy Spirit?

2. Why do some people believe they are Christians because they do good works and appear to be Christians?

3. Why do some people believe they are Christians because they have a relative who is a Christian?

REWARDS

Jesus gives heavenly rewards to believers at the judgment for service they have performed on earth (Matthew 16:27). Rewards are earned; by contrast, salvation is a gift and cannot be earned.

Jesus said a believer can earn rewards for various acts done for other believers. These do not have to be big or complex deeds; they can be very simple deeds. Jesus said that for receiving a prophet or a righteous man, you will get a prophet's or a righteous man's reward, and that is an incentive for helping God's people (Matthew 10:40–42). God wants believers to care for and help each other, which builds bonds of fellowship. When nonbelievers see the way believers care for each other, they may want to become believers too.

Jesus will give believers heavenly rewards for loving their enemies too. Most people are willing to do good for those who do good for them but will not do the same for those who do evil things to them. Believers must be different and will be rewarded for being different. Believers should be willing to do good to both fellow believers and the lost and so to be as perfect as their heavenly Father is perfect (Matthew 5:43–48).

Jesus will give believers heavenly rewards for helping people from their wealth. It's not their wealth; it is God's wealth. We are stewards of his wealth. Jesus wants believers to be willing to sell their possessions so they can give their wealth to the needy. How they spend God's wealth says where their hearts are. Wealth is temporal and is lost as soon as it is found. Thieves break in and steal it, and it gets used up on selfish desires. Believers get heavenly rewards for sharing their wealth with others for the building up of the kingdom of God (Luke 12:33–34).

Jesus will give believers heavenly rewards for not excluding the poor, the crippled, the lame, and the blind. It is easy to provide a service for those who have provided for them and can repay them later, but Jesus wants believers to give to those who will not be able to repay them in this life (Luke 14:12).

Jesus will give believers heavenly rewards for doing their good deeds in private. In fact, if you do your good deeds to gain public acclaim, you will not get a heavenly reward because you will have already received your temporal reward in full. That temporal reward may be in the form of praises or prizes that man gives to you (Matthew 6:1–4).

Jesus will give believers heavenly rewards for fasting in private. Jesus does not want believers to look somber or disheveled when they are fasting. If they do, they will not get a reward in heaven because they will have already received a temporal reward in full from man. So Jesus says that believers should prepare their appearance so people do not know they are fasting (Matthew 6:16–18).

Jesus will give believers heavenly rewards for enduring persecution. Believers should be ready and willing to endure persecution for Christ because that is the same way the prophets before them were treated. Believers will be hated, excluded, insulted, and rejected by nonbelievers. No one wants to be treated this way, but this is the reality for believers who are unafraid to obey God's plan for their lives. Jesus paid the ultimate price for obeying God's plan; believers should be willing to pay the same. Believers must be willing to lose their temporal lives to gain eternal life with God. For doing this, they will be given eternal rewards (Matthew 5:11–12).

Discussion Questions

1. Are heavenly rewards earned, or are they a gift?

2. When are heavenly rewards paid?

3. Why should believers get rewards for loving their enemies?

4. Will believers receive a reward for enduring persecution?

PRAYER

❧

Prayer is talking with God and making your needs and wants known to him.

Jesus said that believers should remain in him and he would remain in them. Remaining in him means trusting and obeying God's plan. Jesus said that he would remain in them i.e., working in and through them, producing the fruit he desires. God will work through believers if they trust and obey his plan. If believers do their part, he will do his part, and whatever believers ask for in prayer will be given to them. That is the key to answered prayer: trusting and obeying God's plan. If people trust and obey their own plans, Jesus said that it would be like a branch that is cut off and thrown away and withers because it did not allow the life-giving power of the Holy Spirit to flow through it. Those withered branches are like people who did not trust and obey God's plan, and on Judgment Day, they will be thrown into the fire of hell for all eternity (John 15:1–17).

Jesus's disciples asked him how to pray, and he taught them a prayer that is commonly called the Lord's Prayer. It's not meant to be a prayer that you recite but one that lets you know what can be asked for in prayer, such as daily needs, forgiveness, temptation, and many other needs.

This, then, is how you should pray:

> Our Father in heaven, hallowed be your name, your kingdom come, your will be done, on earth as it is in heaven. Give us today our daily bread. And forgive us our debts, as we also have forgiven our debtors. And

lead us not into temptation, but deliver us from the
evil one.

For if you forgive other people when they sin against you, your
heavenly Father will also forgive you. But if you do not forgive others
their sins, your Father will not forgive your sins (Matthew 6:9–15).

The Bible says that Jesus spent time alone in prayer. With all the
activity happening all around him and his disciples, Jesus still found
time to be alone in prayer. Early morning, when it was still dark,
was his best time for prayer (Mark 1:35). Today, disciples should find
their best time to pray, when they can be alone in a quiet place and
where they would not be interrupted. But Jesus said there are times
when disciples should pray together with other disciples. He said
when two or more pray together, he would be there with them, and
when they agree in prayer, the Father would do whatever they asked
for (Matthew 18:19–20). Of course, that prayer would have to be in
agreement with God's will.

Disciples should always listen to God, try to discern the will of
God, and pray that his will be done (Matthew 26:42).

Jesus taught his disciples they should be persistent in prayer and
not give up when God does not answer their prayers after a short time
has passed. With persistence, God answers their prayers, even after a
long time has passed (Luke 18:1–8).

Sometimes, when believers have an immediate need, God likes
it when believers are bold in their prayers. He likes it when believers
don't give up seeking answers to their prayers. It may feel as if you are
nagging God, but he likes it when you keep asking until you receive
(Luke 11:5–13).

Discussion Questions

1. What is important to having answered prayer?

2. How should the Lord's Prayer be used?

3. What should believers do when God does not answer their prayers right away?

Summary 3

Summary 3

TEACHING THROUGH BAPTISM

Summary 3 chapters are about the new Christian's education and Church sacraments. Immediately after a person becomes a Christian, he or she should find a Christian church, get a Bible, attend a Bible study group of fellow believers who are following God's plan, participate in communion, and be baptized.

Teaching

The person who brought the new Christian to Christ should be the one to help the new Christian find the following resources: a Christian church, a Bible, and a Bible study group. These said resources should be able to teach the new Christian about God's plan. With participation in communion and getting baptized, the new Christian will learn the first basic sacraments of the Church.

Communion

Communion is the service of Christian worship in which bread and wine are shared for a divine purpose. That purpose is the remembrance of Christ's sufferings on the cross so believers would remember the price that he paid so that they could have fellowship with him.

Baptism

Baptism is the Christian ceremony in which the Christian is dipped into and out of water to symbolize Christ's death, burial, and resurrection. In identification with Christ, the believer's old spiritual nature is put to death, buried, and regenerated into a new spiritual nature. Resurrection is vital to the Christian faith because Jesus is the only person who has ever been resurrected from the dead, and Christ promises to resurrect the believer's physical body when the believer goes to heaven.

TEACHING

Jesus taught on various subjects, and most of these subjects are included in various chapters of this book, discussing the who, what, when, and why of the subject. This chapter on teaching discusses the *who* and the *where*.

Jesus taught the Jews in their synagogues, in temple courts, in places near the lake, in the countryside, and in just about everywhere.

Many times, the Bible speaks of Jesus teaching in their synagogues when he was not in Jerusalem (Matthew 4:23) and in the temple courts when he was in Jerusalem (Mark 12:35).

When teaching crowds of people, at the lake near the house or in the countryside, he often spoke using parables (Matthew 13:34-35); but when speaking privately with the disciples, which were a small group of twelve, he spoke using plain language (Mark 4:10–12).

Discussion Questions

1. When in a small group of believers, with which kind of language should disciples teach them?

2. When in a very large audience of believers and unbelievers, with which kind of language should disciples teach them?

Discussion Questions

1. What is important to having answered prayer?

2. How should the Lord's Prayer be used?

3. What should believers do when God does not answer their prayers right away?

COMMUNION

❧

Communion is the coming together of believers and the taking of bread and wine to symbolize the price Jesus paid on the cross. The bread represents Jesus's body, which suffered much during his crucifixion. The wine represents Jesus's blood, which was poured out for many for the forgiveness of sins. Believers should observe this celebration—eat the bread and drink the wine—often to remind themselves of the price that Jesus paid, which brought them salvation (Matthew 26:26–29).

Discussion Question

1. When believers take communion, what are they sharing in common?

BAPTISM

❧

Baptism is important to Jesus. During his ministry, Jesus and his disciples went into the Judean countryside and baptized. Jesus himself did not baptize anyone, but his disciples did (John 3:22, 4:1–2). At the end of his ministry, Jesus gave some final instructions to his disciples. He commanded them to make disciples of all nations and to baptize them in the name of the Father, the Son, and the Holy Spirit (Matthew 28:18–20).

Baptism is a public event where the believer expresses their commitment to repent of their own plan and to follow God's plan. The actual baptism is in water where the believer stands in the water to identify with Jesus's death on the cross, gets dipped into the water to identify with Jesus's burial, and then gets lifted out of the water to identify with Jesus's resurrection from the dead.

A disciple should be baptized soon after they place their faith in Jesus.

Discussion Questions

1. What is the purpose of water baptism?

2. What does water baptism symbolize?

HUMBLENESS THROUGH FORGIVENESS

Jesus wants his disciples to practice humbleness, compassion, love, and forgiveness. Doing this draws unbelievers to the disciple and makes unbelievers more apt to listen to and accept their message of salvation.

Humbleness

Jesus wants his disciples to be humble, not arrogant. Jesus, although he is God, came to serve sinners. He said the highest-ranking disciples in his kingdom were those who served the most and were servants of all.

Compassion

Compassion begins with a feeling that later turns into an act of kindness. Jesus demonstrated what Christians should do: that is, when a person needed mercy, he did not delay in meeting his or her need. He used what he had to meet that need or accomplished it with a miracle, if necessary. Today's Christians are to do the same.

Love

Jesus said the greatest commandment was to love God and to love others. He said when we begin to love only ourselves, our love grows cold for others. When more of Jesus's disciples practice his kind of love, more love will exist in this world. He said there are rewards in heaven for those who practice his kind of love for their enemies.

Forgiveness

Forgiveness is where the victim of sin pardons the sinner; this brings about reconciliation. First, God wants the sinner to confess and repent of his or her sin. Second, God wants the victim to forgive the sinner. If the sinner will not confess or repent, God will judge and punish the sinner so justice will be accomplished. Forgiveness is not easy. Peter asked Jesus how many times he would have to forgive the sinner, and Jesus said, "Every time." Victims should forgive the sinner, and that amount of forgiveness will be measured unto them (Luke 6:37-38).

HUMBLENESS

Believers should have humble attitudes and seek ways to serve others, which attracts people to them.

Although Jesus is Lord, he did not come to be served but to serve others. In this world, the persons of higher position use that authority to get people of lower position to serve them, but in God's kingdom, believers must be humble and be willing to serve others, no matter their positions in life (Mark 10:42–45).

Because the disciples believed that Jesus was the Messiah and that they were his closest disciples, they believed that they had high ranks in his kingdom. They began to argue about who among the twelve had the highest rank under Jesus. Jesus told his disciples not to argue over who was the greatest in his kingdom. He told them that the greatest or first in his kingdom must be the very last and be the servant of all (Mark 9:33–35). Disciples should not see their positions as greater than others. They should look for ways to serve others at home, at work, or at play. The ones who serve the most will be the highest in Jesus' kingdom.

Disciples should not be afraid to associate with people who are perceived as having low reputations, such as sinners and tax collectors, but should be humble and associate with them, even if it causes damage to their reputations. Jesus associated with sinners without regard to his reputation because he knew that to reach the lost with his message of salvation, he had to associate with them.

By having dinner at Matthew's house and eating with Matthew's "sinner" friends, Jesus showed by example that disciples should associate with sinners because they are the ones believers are sent to save. Jesus said, "It is not the healthy who need a doctor, but the sick"

(Matthew 9:12). Jesus also said, "I desire mercy, not sacrifice. For I have not come to call the righteous, but sinners" (Matthew 9:9–13). In other words, Jesus wants disciples who show mercy more than those who appear to follow the law religiously. Remember, no one is able to keep the law in real life, so trying to appear to follow the law for appearance's sake is not what Jesus wants. He wants disciples who understand and practice mercy.

Although Jesus knew he was the Messiah and was worthy of worship, he showed his disciples, by washing their feet, that they should be willing to serve others, even by taking up the role of the lowest of servants to meet the needs of others (John 13:3–17).

Jesus taught his disciples by using contrasts: pride versus humbleness. Disciples should be humble, as opposed to proud and self-righteous. Disciples are not perfect people; they are sinners, saved only by grace. If not for grace, they would be destined for eternal punishment because they still miss the mark. Self-righteous people who believe they are saved because of their good works will be humbled on Judgment Day. Disciples who are humble will be exalted on Judgment Day (Luke 18:9–14).

In summary, disciples should serve others with humble and not arrogant attitudes. Disciples need to attract people, not repel them, so that people will be willing to hear and consider the disciples' message of salvation.

Discussion Questions

1. What attitude should believers have to attract unbelievers to themselves?

2. What did Jesus tell the twelve about who is the greatest in his kingdom?

3. Why should believers associate with sinners?

4. What did Jesus do to show the twelve they should be willing to serve others?

5. Why should a believer be humble, as opposed to proud and self-righteous?

COMPASSION

Jesus does not want a disciple's offerings or sacrifices to God when they are given out of ritual or hypocrisy. He wants disciples to demonstrate the fruit of the Holy Spirit: love, joy, peace, patience, kindness, goodness, faithfulness, gentleness, and self-control. Even when Jesus's disciples were criticized by the Pharisees for breaking the law by picking and eating heads of grain on the Sabbath because they were hungry, Jesus defended his disciples because it was more important that, through mercy and compassion, their immediate needs be satisfied than to ritualistically obey the law of God (Matthew 12:1–8).

Jesus criticized the teachers of the law and the Pharisees for not practicing mercy and compassion, although they were religious about tithing. Now, tithing is good, but to practice it hypocritically is bad when you pass up immediate opportunities to practice mercy and compassion (Matthew 23:23).

There are many instances in the Bible when people in need asked Jesus to have mercy on them, and he stopped what he was doing and met their needs and many times with a miracle. The important part is that Jesus immediately met their needs. He did not deny or delay their requests (Matthew 20:29–34). Sometimes, disciples have other means to help resolve the problem, including money, time, and other resources. All believers' resources come from God; they are merely stewards of his resources. Believers have freely received, and they should freely give. As believers give, God will refill their supplies. Sometimes, this sharing of mercy leads to salvation and new followers of God.

The key to mercy, compassion, and pity is that it starts with an attitude and leads to an action, which sometimes results in salvation and faith in God. God wants his disciples not only to have Christian habits but to live lives full of random acts of kindness.

Discussion Questions

1. What does Jesus want instead of hypocritical adherence to Jewish rules and regulation?

2. When did Jesus show compassion upon those who asked for it?

3. How should disciples show compassion upon those who ask for it?

LOVE

Disciples are to obey God's plan, and when they do, it shows their love for God—the Father and the Son. God will love them, and Jesus will show himself to them (John 14:21). It all starts with obedience to God and his plan. We can know God through accepting Jesus as our Savior, and we can get to know him better by obeying him as Lord.

Those who are not disciples do not know or love God, and it shows because they do not obey God or his plan. Jesus said that in the last days, there will be an increase in sin, which is disobedience to God. Most people will become lovers of themselves and obey the cravings of their flesh; they will neglect the needs and wants of others. In other words, their love for others will grow cold (Matthew 24:12).

Love for God and others is important for the world because it takes into account the vertical relationship with God and the horizontal relationships with others (Mark 12:28–31). Vertically, God is the Creator and has given believers every good thing that this world has to offer. They should love, obey, and worship him for that. Horizontally, when there are more disciples, there are more people expressing God's kind of love with others. The world cannot express this kind of unconditional love because it is not within them. Individuals need to have God living within them to express God's kind of love with others.

The Golden Rule says believers should do to others what they would have others do to them (Matthew 7:12). This is a horizontal and proactive kind of love. Most religions teach a kind of love that says, "Don't do to others what you don't want done to you." It is more challenging to be proactive in looking for ways to do good to others rather than try to keep from doing bad things to others.

CHUCK BROWN

There are many ways to express this horizontal kind of love. Many days believers are presented with impromptu opportunities they can use to help someone in need. On other days, they can purposefully plan opportunities to do some good. Either way, God commands believers to love their neighbor as they love themselves. Jesus said that when believers help others, they are helping him. The following verses give us some ideas for helping others.

When the Son of Man comes in his glory, and all the angels with him, he will sit on his glorious throne. All the nations will be gathered before him, and he will separate the people one from another as a shepherd separates the sheep from the goats. He will put the sheep on his right and the goats on his left.

> Then the King will say to those on his right, "Come, you who are blessed by my Father; take your inheritance, the kingdom prepared for you since the creation of the world. For I was hungry and you gave me something to eat, I was thirsty and you gave me something to drink, I was a stranger and you invited me in, I needed clothes and you clothed me, I was sick and you looked after me, I was in prison and you came to visit me."
>
> Then the righteous will answer him, "Lord, when did we see you hungry and feed you, or thirsty and give you something to drink? When did we see you a stranger and invite you in, or needing clothes and clothe you? When did we see you sick or in prison and go to visit you?"
>
> The King will reply, "Truly I tell you, whatever you did for one of the least of these brothers and sisters of mine, you did for me." (Matthew 25:31–40)

Believers are to love their enemies too. This is not the kind of love where you have affection toward the person loved. This is the unconditional love that God shares with everyone every day (Matthew 5:43–45).

You are to do good to your enemies, and by forgiving them for doing bad things to you, you will be rewarded in heaven (Luke 6:35–36). The bottom line for disciples is that they are to represent God and be loving and merciful to their enemies.

Discussion Questions

1. How does a disciple show his or her love for God?

2. Why will the love of most people grow cold?

3. What did Jesus say was the most important commandment?

4. What are some ways to obey the Golden Rule?

5. Why should disciples love their enemies to be like representatives of God?

FORGIVENESS

❧

Forgiveness occurs when the victim of sin pardons the sinner; this brings about reconciliation. God does not want people sinning against each other, but when they do, God wants sinners to confess and repent of their sins; then God wants the victim to forgive the sinner (Luke 17:3–4). If the sinner will not confess or repent, God will judge and punish the sinner so justice is accomplished. Forgiveness is not easy. Peter asked Jesus how many times he would have to forgive the sinner, and Jesus said every time (Matthew 18:21–22). Victims should forgive the sinner, and that amount of forgiveness will be measured unto them (Matthew 7:1–2).

Within Church discipline, if a believer sins against another believer, a certain protocol is to be followed. The victim is to rebuke the person who sinned, in private. If the sinner repents, then forgiveness should occur. If that sinner does not repent, then the victim is to bring one or two other witnesses, and if the sinner still does not repent, then the victim should bring the situation to the church. And if the sinner does not repent, then he or she should be treated as an outsider or an unbeliever (Matthew 18:15–17).

Discussion Questions

1. How many times are believers to forgive a sinner?

2. When should believers rebuke a sinner?

3. What is the protocol for church discipline?

Summary 5

MONEY THROUGH DEATH

Summary 5 chapters are about God's provision. God provides monetary resources, guidance, protection, healing, and revival from death.

Money

When the believers' resources are insufficient for the situation, God wants them to use what they have and, by faith, trust him to provide the rest.

When their own efforts have not provided what they need, they need to listen to God and try again, and he will make their efforts more fruitful.

When God does provide, he provides what the believer needs or better.

Guidance

Jesus told his disciples that the Holy Spirit would guide them into all truth. Today, when believers need guidance, they should study their Bibles to know what to do for the situation and move in that direction; then, when God has more information, he will share it so believers can change direction, if that is needed.

Protection

Jesus provides the believer with eternal protection from life's trouble when the believer follows God's plan. However, the unbeliever does not receive this kind of protection because the unbeliever does not follow God's plan.

Healing

Jesus healed people of all kinds of ailments. Believers can do the same as Jesus's representatives if they have faith and pray. "Everything is possible for him who believes" (Mark 9:23).

Death

Jesus raised people from the dead. He would command the dead individual to get up, and he or she would do so. Sometimes, Jesus said, the dead person's advocate's faith healed the dead person.

MONEY

❧

Jesus showed his disciples how God works miracles to provide for large immediate financial needs.

When disciples are faced with a financial need that is larger than their on-hand resources, Jesus wants them, through faith, to use what they have and trust him to provide the rest. Jesus performed a miracle when he multiplied the financial resources to meet the said large immediate need. The end result was that God generously met that need and provided more financial resources than what was originally on hand. The example is when Jesus fed the five thousand with only five loaves of bread and two fish (Matthew 14:15–21).

When his disciples had been trying to meet their financial needs on their own strength and were unsuccessful, Jesus directed them to try again, and this time, through obedience and faith, their efforts were successful. They caught such a large number of fish that their nets began to break and their boats began to sink (Luke 5:4–7).

When God provides, he does not provide low-quality resources; he provides the same or better resources than what were originally supplied. The example is when Jesus turned water into wine at a wedding. His wine was better than what the host had originally supplied (John 2:1–11).

Discussion Questions

1. When believers have been unfruitful in their efforts or do not have enough financial resources to meet an immediate need, what should they do?

2. When God provides financial resources, what quality or quantity of resources does he provide?

GUIDANCE

❧

Jesus said he would leave the disciples and send them the Holy Spirit to guide them in his absence. The Spirit would teach them all things and remind them of everything he had told them about God's plan (John 14:26).

Jesus used two names for the Holy Spirit: *Counselor* and *Spirit of truth* (John 15:26). The term Counselor refers to the Spirit's role in providing, teaching, and remembrance.

Jesus said the Spirit would guide the disciples into all truth heard from Jesus and the Father (John 16:13–15). To share this truth about God's plan, the disciples would need guidance in speaking before everyone, including rulers and authorities (Luke 12:11–12).

Discussion Question

1. What does the Holy Spirit do to help disciples in fulfilling God's plan?

PROTECTION

❧

Jesus asked God to protect his disciples from Satan. Today disciples should ask God for protection from Satan too, but they should not ask God to take them out of the world; they are here for God's purposes (John 17:11–15). God will take them out of the world according to his own timing.

When the storms of life affect believers and unbelievers, there are different outcomes. Believers withstand the difficulty and do not crash and fall because of their faith in God. They believe that they are under God's eternal protection for following God's plan. Unbelievers, however, crash and fall because of their lack of faith in God. They are unsure of whether their plan will give them eternal protection. Believers know that even death cannot take away their eternal life with God. Because the temporal environment is Satan's domain; he can cause disciples temporal harm, but he cannot cause them eternal harm. As long as they follow Jesus, he will protect them from the storms of life (Matthew 7:24–27).

Speaking of storms, the disciples found themselves in a physical storm that caused great waves to wash over their boat and threaten their very lives. Jesus was with them in the boat, sleeping. They were so afraid that they went to Jesus to save them and woke him up. He criticized the disciples for having little faith. Jesus rebuked the waves, and the water became calm. Today, when disciples find themselves facing physical or spiritual danger, they should remember to fear not and to trust God to protect them. If they have been trusting God and following God's plan for their lives, they can expect God to protect them (Matthew 8:23–27).

Jesus is the believers' protector. He protects believers from bad circumstances and bad people. Jesus provides eternal protection by providing eternal life. No one else can provide eternal life and protection; only Jesus can do so.

Discussion Questions

1. From whom does Jesus want to protect his disciples?

2. Why should believers not be afraid when facing the storms of life?

HEALING

❧

Jesus healed people with all kinds of ailments: leprosy, demonic possession, paralysis, bleeding, blindness, muteness, deafness, fever, a shriveled hand, and others. The key factor in each of the healings was faith. Disciples should have faith and remember who they are when they try to help heal a person. They are representatives of God, with the authority to perform miracles in Jesus's name as God works through them (Mark 9:14–29).

There were times when Jesus said that the person being healed had "great faith." For example, when a centurion came to him, asking him to heal his servant, Jesus wanted to go to the centurion's home to heal the servant, but the centurion said Jesus did not have to go to his house. All Jesus had to do was say the word, and the servant would be healed. That's great faith in Jesus's authority to heal (Matthew 8:5–10).

Another example is the time when a gentile Canaanite woman came to Jesus and asked for healing for her daughter, who had suffered terribly from demonic possession. Jesus did not heal her right away; he stated that the Jews were worthy of God's healing because they were God's children, not gentiles. The woman persisted, however, saying that even "dogs" (another name for gentiles) were allowed to be healed, as if they were getting "seconds" that had fallen from the master's table. Jesus admired her great faith and healed her daughter that very hour (Matthew 15:21–28).

Discussion Questions

1. What should a disciple have in order to be used by God to heal someone?

2. What does Jesus say about those who have "great faith"?

3. What does a disciple need in order to work miracles in Jesus's name?

DEATH

❧

Jesus raised people from the dead. He is God, and therefore, he has the authority to raise people from the dead. He would touch the dead person and that person would get up, or he would speak a command; for example, "Little girl, I say to you, get up!" Another time, he said, "Young man, I say to you, get up!" (Mark 5:38–42, Luke 7:11–15).

The person who came to Jesus on the dead person's behalf spoke words of faith; for example, "My daughter has just died. But come and put your hand on her, and she will live" (Matthew 9:18). On another occasion, Jesus told the dead person's advocate, "Don't be afraid, just believe, and she will be healed" (Luke 8:50).

As God's representatives, disciples have the authority to wake a person from the dead, if God wills it to be done.

Discussion Questions

1. What does a disciple need to have and do in order to raise a person from the dead?

2. Besides the disciples, who needs to have faith in order to help raise a person from the dead?

Summary 6

INCARNATION THROUGH RETURN

Summary 6 chapters are about Jesus being the Messiah. All the chapters—incarnation, miracles, atonement, resurrection, and return—say that he is the Messiah.

Incarnation

Jesus is the Messiah because he is the literal Son of God; that is, God was his Father, Mary was his mother, and Joseph was his stepfather. Because Jesus is both God and man, he is sinless; he was born that way. No other religion has a founder who was born this way. This makes Christianity unique.

Miracles

Jesus's miracles proved that he was the Messiah. The Jews, disciples, and demons all had firsthand experiences with Jesus performing miracles. Miracles still happen today because God is the same God that worked them in biblical times. God wants to reveal himself, and he will, through miracles.

Atonement

Jesus is the Messiah because he made atonement for people's sins when he shed his blood and died on a cross while being crucified for their sins. His atonement for sin made it possible for people to be reconciled to God.

Resurrection

Jesus proved he was the Messiah through his resurrection from the dead. After Jesus's death on the cross, he was placed into a tomb, where he lay for three days. On the third day, Jesus raised himself from the dead and appeared to the disciples, the women, and others. He is the only person who ever has been resurrected from the dead. No founder of any other religion in the world has ever been raised from the dead.

Ascension

Before Jesus ascended into heaven, he told his disciples he would send the Holy Spirit from heaven to comfort and guide them. When the time finally came for his ascension, Jesus led the disciples to a place in the vicinity of Bethany, where he left them physically and was taken up into heaven.

Return

The Bible describes Jesus's return as him sitting on his throne, coming on the clouds of the sky with power and great glory and with his angels. The event will be visible to all the inhabitants of the earth. Unbelievers will mourn because they will realize they made the wrong decision by refusing to accept Jesus as their Savior and Lord and that it was too late to change their minds.

INCARNATION

❦

Before the creation of heaven and earth, Jesus existed with God. In fact, Jesus is God (John 1:1–3). Jesus is eternal; he has no beginning or ending. He knew, before the creation of the world, that individuals would fall into sin and need salvation from God's judgment. He knew that individuals would need a Savior to accomplish this salvation. Only God is sinless, and so he had to be the Savior. At the right time, the incarnation of Jesus took place (i.e., God assumed human form) (John 1:14).

God chose a virgin named Mary and a carpenter named Joseph to be the mother and stepfather for the child Jesus. Joseph was the stepfather because God was Jesus's father. When the angel told Mary that she was going to be a mother, Mary asked him how this would happen, as she was a virgin. The angel told her how the Holy Spirit would overshadow her so that the child Jesus would be uniquely called the Son of God. Jesus is both fully human and fully God because Mary is his mother and God is his father (Matthew 1:18-23); thus, Jesus was born without a sin nature.

Disciples need to believe in the virgin birth because no other religion has a founder and leader who was born this way. This makes Christianity unique.

Discussion Questions

1. Why is it important that the Savior needed to be God?

2. How is it that Jesus is both God and man?

MIRACLES

Jesus's miracles proved that he was the Messiah. The Jews, disciples, and demons all had firsthand experiences with Jesus performing miracles.

The Jews, who had seen Jesus perform many miracles, did not believe he was the Christ even though he had plainly said he was the Christ. The Jews, understanding that Jesus had claimed to be God, wanted to stone him because they believed what he had said was blasphemous (John 10:22–33).

Jesus demonstrated to the Jews he was the Christ through the miraculous healing and the forgiving of the sins of the paralytic. Once again, the Jews wanted to stone him for blasphemy because he forgave someone's sins, something only God could do (Mark 2:1–12).

The disciples witnessed the miracle of Jesus walking on the water and leading Peter to do the same. After seeing this, the disciples in the boat worshipped Jesus, saying, "Truly you are the Son of God" (Matthew 14:25-33).

Demons are not friends of Christ and do not worship him either, but they know who he is—the Son of God. Because of Jesus's authority over them, they have to obey him. Jesus performed miracles of rebuking and casting out demons (Luke 4:33–36, 41; Mark 3:11).

Disciples need to know, believe, and obey God's plan so God will work miraculously through them to accomplish his will. Miracles still happen today because God is the same God who worked them in biblical times. God wants to reveal himself, and he will—through miracles.

Discussion Questions

1. Why did the Jews not believe that Jesus was God, even after witnessing the miracles?

2. Why should disciples believe that God performs miracles today?

3. Why do disciples have authority over demons?

ATONEMENT

Jesus made atonement for people's sins when he shed his blood and died on a cross while being crucified for their sins. His atonement for sin made it possible for people to become forgiven and reconciled to God.

Jesus's death on the cross always was a central part of God's plan from the beginning of time and was prophesized by prophets in the Old Testament. Jesus explained this to the twelve, but they did not understand because the meaning of his death was hidden from them (Luke 18:31–34).

Jesus spoke of the purpose of the atonement in his teaching about communion. He said that communion, involving his body and blood, demonstrated the new covenant between God and man. The old covenant involved animal sacrifices, with the spilling of blood of a spotless lamb. The new covenant involved the sacrifice and shedding of blood of the sinless Lamb of God: Jesus Christ. The atonement under the new covenant is made effective by repentance from sin and faith in Jesus Christ as the Messiah (Matthew 26:26–29).

Under the old covenant within the temple, there were three areas: the courts, the holy place, and the most holy place. A curtain separated the holy place from the most holy place. The most holy place was where the high priest entered only once per year to atone for the sins of the people. On the day that Jesus was crucified, when he cried out, "It is finished," the curtain was torn in two from top to bottom, the earth shook, and the rocks split. The centurion—who was standing near Jesus, heard Jesus's last words, and saw him give up his spirit—said, "Surely this man was the Son of God." Jesus's statement, "It is finished," means to be paid in full, signifying the end of the need for the old covenant sacrifices (Mark 15:37–39; John 19:30).

Before his arrest, Jesus explained to the disciples that he was going to be betrayed by the chief priests and teachers of the law, who would condemn him to death and hand him over to the gentiles. The gentiles would mock him, spit on him, flog him, and kill him; three days later, he would rise from the dead. After hearing Jesus explain this, the disciples were filled with grief and despair (Matthew 17:22-23). So when Jesus told them he was going to die and be resurrected, they did not understand. They only heard the part about his dying and could not understand that his death and resurrection would bring victory over sin and make his kingdom possible. In almost every verse in which Jesus talked about his death, he also spoke of his resurrection. The disciples had never experienced a resurrection before and did not understand it until after Jesus's resurrection; then they understood that his death and resurrection would bring victory and hope.

Jesus told his disciples that his death would be like a kernel of wheat; when it falls to the ground and dies, it remains only a single seed, but after it is buried, it sprouts a blade of wheat that produces many more seeds (John 12:23–25). Disciples are the "many more seeds" who die to their selfish sin nature only to be born again and to lead other unbelievers to become believers and experience eternal life.

Discussion Questions

1. What did Jesus's atoning death on the cross accomplish?

2. Why did the disciples not know that Jesus's death and resurrection would bring victory and hope?

RESURRECTION

～

After Jesus's death, the disciples were scared and scattered. They had yet to understand that Jesus's death was part of God's plan for victory. They were scared because they thought that since they were Jesus's disciples, they were next to be put to death, and so they scattered (Matthew 26:31–32).

The story of the resurrection begins with the empty tomb. The chief priests and the Pharisees remembered that Jesus had predicted his resurrection. They went to Pilate and asked him to have the tomb protected from the disciples so the disciples could not make it appear that the resurrection had happened by stealing the body and then claiming it was missing because of the resurrection (Matthew 27:62–66).

Three days after Jesus's death, an angel appeared to the guards and rolled away the stone. Upon seeing this, the guards fainted and later ran away. Mary Magdalene and the other Mary went to look at the tomb and met the angel. He told them Jesus was no longer there and that he had risen. The angel invited them to look into the tomb to verify that what he had told them was true (Matthew 28:1–7). One of the reasons the resurrection is so believable is because of the many firsthand facts and evidence that are stated in the Bible.

After his resurrection, Jesus appeared to many people. The first appearance was to Mary Magdalene (Mark 16:9) and to the other Mary; Matthew 28:5–10).

These women went back to the disciples to tell them of Jesus's appearance, but when the disciples heard what the women told them, they did not believe them (Luke 24:9–11).

Jesus next appeared to two men, one being a man named Cleopas. The two men reported this appearance to the others, but they did not believe them either (Mark 16:12–13).

It was not until Jesus appeared to the disciples, minus Thomas, that they believed he had been resurrected. He showed them the evidence of his wounds (John 20:19-20) (Luke 24:36-40), and he ate some fish in their presence to give them evidence that he was not a spirit (Luke 24:41-43). Jesus went away. Then the disciple named Thomas came back to the place where the disciples stayed. The disciples told Thomas of Jesus's appearance, but he said he would not believe them unless he saw Jesus with his own eyes. Later, Jesus appeared to Thomas and let him touch his wounds, and then Thomas believed (John 20:24–29).

Believers and unbelievers should believe in the resurrection because of all of the firsthand evidence presented in the Bible. Because of the resurrection, disciples can believe Jesus is the promised Messiah and his death on the cross can atone for the sins of everyone. Not every person will believe, in spite of the evidence, and disciples should continue to share God's plan to all unbelievers so they can see and experience God's love through his disciples.

Discussion Questions

1. After Jesus's death, what were the chief priests and the Pharisees afraid of?

2. What caused the guard to faint and then to run away?

3. What are some of the firsthand facts and evidence of Jesus's resurrection?

4. What was the disciples' first reaction to hearing about Jesus's resurrection?

5. What was the disciples' reaction to Jesus's resurrection after seeing and touching him?

ASCENSION

❧

Jesus predicted to his disciples that he would leave them and then come back to them. He did this so that when it did happen, it would cause his disciples to believe in him even more; it would be another prediction that came true, like his resurrection from the dead (John 14:28–29).

Before his ascension into heaven, Jesus told his disciples that he would send the Holy Spirit from heaven to comfort and guide them. Just as Jesus had been with them physically (limited to being in one place at a time), the Holy Spirit would be with them, with no limits on how many places he could be at the same time. The Holy Spirit could be anywhere and everywhere at the same time. The Holy Spirit, the Spirit of truth, would guide them into all truth. He would know everything that Jesus knows and would be able to tell them of future things to come (John 14:15–20; 16:5–16).

When the time finally came for his ascension, Jesus led the disciples to a place in the vicinity of Bethany and left them, physically, and was taken up into heaven. Now, the disciples were not filled with grief but were filled with great joy, and they were continually at the temple, praising God (Luke 24:50–53).

Discussion Questions

1. Why did Jesus tell his disciples he was going to go away and then return?

2. What would the Holy Spirit do after Jesus had ascended?

RETURN

❧

The Bible clearly states that Jesus is the Son of God, the Messiah, when talking about his return to earth after his ascension into heaven. The Bible describes his return as Jesus sitting on his throne, coming back on the clouds of the sky, with power and great glory and with his angels (Matthew 25:31). The event will be visible for all of the inhabitants of earth to see, just as lightning that comes from the east is visible even in the west (Matthew 24:27). And unbelievers will mourn because they will realize that they made the wrong choice and that it is too late to change their minds (Matthew 24:30).

Immediately before Jesus's return, there will be signs in the sky: the sun will become dark, the moon will not give its light, stars will fall from the sky, and the heavenly bodies will be shaken (Mark 13:24–26; Luke 21:25–28). People will faint from terror, fearing what is coming on the world.

No one knows the date or time of his return, not even the angels or Jesus; only the Father knows. But when Jesus does return, people will be doing normal activities, just like people were doing in Noah's day, just before the flood. They will be eating and drinking, marrying and giving in marriage. Also, believers will be taken mysteriously, called the Rapture. It will be like two people, a believer and an unbeliever, working together, and the believer will be taken, and the unbeliever will be left behind. Remember that salvation is a free offer, but it is a limited-time offer. When Jesus returns, it will be too late to take him up on that free offer. You must be ready because Jesus will return at a time when you do not expect him (Matthew 24:36–42).

Jesus wants his disciples to be ready when he returns. He wants them to be working God's plan until the day they die or Jesus returns. If disciples think that Jesus is taking a long time to return and begin to live like unbelievers, woe be unto them. Jesus will assign them places in hell instead of heaven (Luke 12:35-46). After salvation, it is very important that new believers receive discipleship to learn and obey God's plan for the rest of their lives so they can live with confidence that eternal life with God is theirs, for now and forever.

Discussion Questions

1. How would you describe Jesus's return?

2. Who knows the timing of Jesus's return?

3. What will unbelievers be doing when Jesus returns?

4. What will disciples be doing when Jesus returns?

DISOBEDIENCE THROUGH ETERNAL LIFE

Summary 7 chapters are about whether or not a person can get into heaven by disobeying God's plan and following their own plan, even if it includes doing good works. Disobedience to God's plan leads a person to hell, while obedience to God's plan leads a person to heaven. Doing good works does not allow a person to escape going to hell; only faith in Jesus Christ as Savior and Lord allows a person to have eternal life. Eternal life is where believers go, by grace, to live in heaven with God and his angels for all eternity. In contrast, hell is where unbelievers go to live in hell with Satan and his demons for all eternity.

Disobedience

Sins are caused by disobeying God's plan. For unbelievers, there is a problem: their sins are recorded in their personal record books. On

Judgment Day, God will see those sins and will find the unbelievers guilty and send them to hell for all eternity. For believers, there is no problem. On Judgment Day, God will look at their personal record books and find no sins, because they have been forgiven, and find the believers innocent and send them to heaven for all eternity.

Judgment

On Judgement Day unbelievers will be sent to hell, and believers will be sent to heaven. Hell is described as a place of terrible pain for Satan and his followers. Heaven is described as a place of physical and spiritual perfection for God and his followers. The question for everyone is, where do you want to spend eternity? It's a choice each person must make.

Good Works

Good works are good deeds that make things better for people. Unbelievers believe that if their good works exceed their sins, they will be able to get into heaven. Salvation does not work that way. Salvation is by faith alone in Jesus Christ as Savior and Lord. Jesus called the Jews, who believed that following their rules and traditions to get them into heaven, hypocrites.

Eternal Life

Eternal life is obtained as a gift, not from doing good works. Eternal life is where you spend eternity with God, angels, and believers. Eternal punishment is where you spend eternity with Satan, demons, and unbelievers. Eternal life involves three steps; the first step is called justification, the second step is called sanctification, and the third step is called glorification. Each step is covered in more detail in other parts of this book. Justification includes four different theological doctrines: forgiveness, redemption, being born again, and being baptized in the Holy Spirit.

DISOBEDIENCE

For nonbelievers, there is a problem: they have sin on their personal record books. On Judgment Day, God will look at the personal record books, see the sins, pronounce a guilty verdict, and send the nonbeliever to the lake of fire for all eternity.

For believers, there is no problem; they have no sin on their personal record books. On Judgment Day, God will look at their personal record books and see no sins because they have been forgiven. He will pronounce an innocent verdict and send the believers to heaven for all eternity.

During their lives, believers learn to show their love for God by obeying God's plan. They have been saved by repentance and faith in God and can see and understand God's plan. Unbelievers have not been saved, and they do not obey God's plan because they cannot see or understand God's plan; they have their own plans they are following.

Discussion Questions

1. What is the problem for nonbelievers?

2. Why is there no problem for believers?

3. How do individuals show their love for God?

JUDGMENT

❧

There will be two judgments: one for believers and another for unbelievers.

There are certain unbelievers who do not believe in a Judgment Day or in a place called hell. What a surprise is waiting for them. The Bible says all of the dead unbelievers will hear the voice of Jesus and will be raised to face condemnation by him, whether or not they believe in life after death. Some unbelievers believe that life ends when they die here on earth, but that is not true. Believers believe that there will be a Judgment Day, and on that day, they will be judged innocent and sent to heaven (John 5:25–29).

God allows believers and unbelievers to live together here on earth until Judgment Day, and then he will send his angels to collect both. The believers and unbelievers will then be separated from each other. The unbelievers will be condemned and sent to hell, and the believers will be found innocent and sent to heaven (Matthew 13:24–30).

How bad will hell be? How is it described in the Bible? It is described as a lake of fire, an unquenchable fire, a place where the worm does not die, a fiery furnace where there will be weeping and gnashing of teeth. It is really bad because it was created for the punishment of the devil and his demons. Heaven is really good because it was created for life with God, his angels, and believers (Mark 9:43–48; Matthew 13:36–43).

Good fruit is the result of obeying God's plan, with the help of the Holy Spirit. Anyone who does not produce good fruit will be thrown into the lake of fire. Believers who obey God's plan will produce good fruit. Unbelievers who do not obey God's plan will not produce good fruit and will be condemned to the lake of fire (Matthew 3:8–10; John 15:4–6).

Because of the aforementioned, everyone has an incentive to follow God's plan. The question is, where do you want to spend eternity? The answer is simple: heaven. Remember that salvation is by grace through faith in Jesus as your Savior. Rewards are earned by obeying God's plan through the power of the Holy Spirit, with Jesus as your Lord.

Discussion Questions

1. How should unbelievers feel about Judgment Day?

2. How should believers feel about Judgment Day?

3. What happens to the kind of branch that bears good fruit, and what happens to the kind of branch that does not bear good fruit?

GOOD WORKS

❧

Unbelievers have a sin problem, and that problem keeps them from receiving eternal life. They think they can resolve this problem by doing good works. They hope they can do enough good works to outweigh their sins and earn a place in heaven, but God's judgment does not work that way. God looks at your personal record book, and if he sees even one sin, he will judge you guilty and send you to hell for all eternity, no matter how many good works you have done. Your own righteousness, by way of not doing bad works and of doing good works, will not get you into heaven (Luke 18:9–14).

Some unbelievers will be surprised when they come before God on Judgment Day and find that their good works did not save them from going to hell. They did not have a relationship with Jesus, did not accept him as Savior, and did not obey him as Lord (Matthew 7:21–23).

Jesus called some Pharisees and teachers of the law hypocrites because they placed their man-made traditions and rules as equal to God's Word. God says obeying these traditions and rules is doing good works in vain because they cannot be used to offset their sins. God wants believers to put their faith in him for salvation and to obey his plan, not man's plan (Mark 7:1–8).

Some unbelievers want to know what good works they must do to get eternal life. Jesus says they have to obey the commandments. But because of humans' sinful nature, it is natural for humans to sin, get sins recorded in their personal record books, and thus be disqualified from obtaining eternal life (Matthew 19:16-17).

Some unbelievers may ask, "What is the point of doing good works if they will not get you eternal life?" Jesus said that first you must be saved, and then your good works will be rewarded in heaven. Good works alone do not get you eternal life. Eternal life is by grace through faith in Jesus Christ as your Savior.

Some unbelievers may ask, "What good work can a person do to resolve the sin problem?" and "What good works does God require?" The answer is this: to do the work that God requires is to believe in Jesus Christ as your Savior (John 6:28–29).

Discussion Questions

1. What good are good works if they do not get you into heaven?

2. Under what condition do good works get rewarded in heaven?

3. What did Jesus say about doing good works that get you into heaven?

ETERNAL LIFE

Eternal life is by grace through faith, not works. Eternal life is a gift because Jesus did all the work and offers it to us as a free gift when we place our faith in him as our Savior (John 3:16).

Eternal life is where you spend eternity with God in heaven, if you have put your faith in Jesus Christ. Eternal punishment is where you spend your eternity with Satan in hell if you have refused to put your faith in Jesus.

Jesus is the Savior of the entire world. The Samaritans learned this from listening to the testimony of the Samaritan woman who met Jesus at the well and then again from listening to his message firsthand.

Many of the Samaritans from that town believed in him because of the woman's testimony: "He told me everything I ever did." So, when the Samaritans came to him, they urged him to stay with them, and he stayed two days. And because of his words, many more became believers.

They said to the woman, "We no longer believe just because of what you said; now we have heard for ourselves, and we know that this man really is the Savior of the world" (John 4:39–42).

Eternal life involves three steps; the first step is called justification, the second step is called sanctification, and the third step is called glorification. Each step is covered in more detail in other parts of this book. When a new believer experiences eternal life the first step, justification occurs, which includes several doctrinal experiences: redemption, forgiveness, being born again, and being baptized in the Holy Spirit. These all occur at once when they place their faith in Jesus. Forgiveness frees them from being found guilty of sins. Redemption frees them from being slaves to their sin nature. Being born again creates a new spirit and makes it possible for them to receive the Holy Spirit. The baptism of the Holy Spirit empowers them to work God's plan with power.

First, let's talk about forgiveness. The remedy for sins being recorded in our personal books in heaven is forgiveness. Forgiveness occurs because of Jesus's death on the cross. All sins are taken from the books and laid on Jesus. He died to pay the price for those sins so they would be forgiven. For those who put their faith in him, their personal records are cleared of all sins.

Second, let's talk about redemption. The remedy for being slaves to sin is redemption. Everyone is born a slave to sin, which leads him or her to commit sins. Individuals' sin nature is the root cause of their problems for committing sins, so much so that the Bible says they are slaves to sin (John 8:34). Redemption occurs because Jesus died on the cross in their places. His death paid the ransom to purchase them out of judgment and eternal punishment in hell (Mark 10:45).

Third, let's talk about being born again. To be born again is to be regenerated with a new spirit. Being born again makes it possible for believers to enter the kingdom of God, to have their spiritual eyes opened so they can satisfy their spiritual thirst and hunger by reading the Word of God, and to experience a relationship with God (John 3:3–5).

Fourth, let's talk about being baptized with the Holy Spirit. John the Baptist said that Jesus was going to be the one who would baptize with the Holy Spirit. And Jesus said that baptism with the Holy Spirit would give the disciples the power needed to work God's plan effectively (Luke 24:49).

That's right—the Holy Spirit would work through the disciples to give them the correct words to say when presenting the Gospel message, receiving revelation as to future events, guidance, teaching, remembrance, etc. (Mark 13:11, John 14:26).

Discussion Questions

1. Why is eternal life by grace through faith?

2. What four things occur when a person experiences eternal life?

3. Why does the Bible say, "Everyone who sins is a slave to sin"?'

REPENTANCE THROUGH FAITH

Summary 8 chapters are about the disciple's decision to accept Jesus as Savior and Lord. It requires repentance and faith to become a believer in Jesus Christ.

Repentance

Before we come to Jesus, we are working our own plans. Our own plans usually consist of doing anything but God's plan. Our plans have to do with self-interests: career, money, hobbies, good works, and so on. These are not bad plans, but they do not lead to eternal life. Working God's plan leads to eternal life. Jesus's first disciples left their businesses to follow Jesus because they believed that following him would lead them to eternal life.

Faith

Eternal life is by grace through faith in Jesus Christ. By grace, God is responsible for making the Gospel message clear to the unbeliever. Then, by faith, it is the unbeliever's responsibility to make the decision to accept or reject the Gospel message. How does an unbeliever express his or her faith in Jesus? Many make a profession of faith through prayer. After saying the prayer, the unbeliever becomes a Christian.

REPENTANCE

Repentance is turning from working your own plan to working God's plan. For unbelievers, working your own plan means working any plan but God's plan. It usually has to do with some self-interest: career, money, hobbies, good works, and so on. These are not bad plans, but only God's plan leads to eternal life. The Bible says that when Jesus called his first disciples, they left their businesses to follow him. They believed that he was the Messiah and were willing to repent of what they were doing to learn God's plan, as taught by Jesus (Matthew 4:18–22). These were hardworking men who heard Jesus talk about eternal life and the need to repent and believe the good news. They decided that was what they wanted to do, and they believed that Jesus knew the plan to get there. I believe that today, Jesus wants his disciples to study and to know him and obey him, repenting of all things that are against and not according to God's plan.

Jesus knows how important material possessions are to people. People worry about having enough, no matter how much or little they think they have. Some people have financial plans to help them to retire and live a life of leisure (Luke 12:16–21). This is not God's plan. God expects disciples to work for him for their entire lives. The problem is not in saving money but in being self-serving. God wants disciples to use their financial resources to meet their own financial needs and to work God's plan. God knows their financial needs and will meet them. He wants them to have their priorities in the correct order. He wants believers first to work God's plan and then have faith that he will continue to meet their daily financial needs. He wants believers to focus on knowing where their true treasure is and to keep working God's plan to increase their eternal rewards (Matthew 6:19–34).

Discussion Questions

1. What is man's plan?

2. What is God's plan?

3. In light of questions 1 and 2, what is repentance?

FAITH

Eternal life is by grace through faith in Jesus Christ. By grace, God is responsible for making the Gospel message clear to the unbeliever, and then, by faith, it is the individual's responsibility to decide whether to accept or reject the Gospel message.

By grace, God is the one who reveals, enables, and draws God's Gospel message to the unbeliever (Luke 10:22; John 6:44, 65). The Gospel message is that Jesus is the Messiah who died on the cross in the believer's place, to deliver him from sin so he could have eternal life with God. Not everyone who hears the message is ready to accept it. Believers are to share the message with as many people as possible because believers are unable to judge whether God has made a person ready or not. Believers can judge only by the decision the unbeliever makes (i.e., whether the unbeliever accepts or rejects the message).

After the believer shares the Gospel message with the unbeliever, the believer should be ready to answer any questions the unbeliever may have and to lead the unbeliever to faith in Jesus. Eternal life is by grace through faith in Jesus Christ. How do unbelievers express their faith in Jesus? Many make a profession of faith through prayer. A prayer of faith in Jesus can be as simple as:

Heavenly Father,

I believe that your Son, Jesus, is the Messiah who died on the cross in my place so that I may have eternal life with you. I accept your free gift and give my life to you to teach me how to live life according to your plan. Amen.

Anyone who sincerely says this prayer becomes a Christian and should immediately find a Christian church, obtain a Bible, join a Bible study group of fellow believers who are following God's plan. Jesus's first disciples joined his group, and he taught them God's plan for the three-plus years of his earthly ministry. But it all began with God's grace, followed by acceptance of the Gospel message through faith. Then discipleship is the natural next step in living life according to God's plan.

Discussion Questions

1. Why is an unbeliever able to understand the Gospel message when it is shared with him or her?

2. What should a new believer do after he or she has become a Christian?

Summary 9

REPRODUCTION—CALLING THROUGH REPRODUCTION - INCREASE

God's plan for Church growth includes reproduction. It starts when the unbeliever hears the Gospel message and is asked to accept Jesus as Savior and Lord; that's the calling. Then, those new believers who remain in Christ—those who do not fall away—are appointed to receive more training; that's the appointment. After more training, those disciples are delegated to go out in small groups, comprised of at least two people, to share the Gospel; this is the delegation. When those teams come back together, they share their experiences and results; this is the accountability. All these steps repeat themselves over and over again causing reproduction; and that's the increase.

Reproduction—Calling

The calling is when, after sharing the Gospel with someone, you ask him or her to accept Jesus as Savior and Lord. People have various reactions to the calling. Some reject the call. Some accept the call but fall away when trouble or persecution occurs. Some accept the call but go back to working their own plan instead of God's plan. Others accept the call, get a Bible, join a Bible study group and a church, and get discipled until they are working God's plan.

Reproduction—Appointment

The appointment is when, after the acceptance of the call and the believer has not fallen away from Christ, he or she is appointed as a disciple to receive more intensive training.

Reproduction—Delegation

The delegation is when, after the disciple has received enough intensive training, he or she is sent out with a team of fellow disciples to share God's plan.

Reproduction—Accountability

The accountability is when the teams return for a group meeting and report their experiences. Each member can learn from the others' experiences, whether good or bad.

Reproduction—Increase

The increase is when the number of disciples in the Church grows; and God wants his Church to grow through one generation discipling the next generation thus causing multiplication.

REPRODUCTION—CALLING

❧

After sharing the Gospel with people, the *calling* is when you ask them to accept Jesus as their Savior and Lord. Some people do not accept Jesus the first time they are called, and sometimes, people do not continue to follow Jesus after making their first acceptance decision. Sometimes, people walk away from following Jesus and go back to doing whatever they were doing before they made their initial acceptance decision.

The first four disciples—Peter, Andrew, John, and James—did not follow Jesus permanently the first time they met him or received their first call. In their first meeting with Jesus, Andrew and John asked if they could spend some time with him, and he let them. Andrew found his brother Peter and introduced him to Jesus.

> The next day, John was there again with two of his disciples. When he saw Jesus passing by, he said, "Look, the Lamb of God!"
>
> When the two disciples heard him say this, they followed Jesus. Turning around, Jesus saw them following and asked, "What do you want?"
>
> They said, "Rabbi" (which means "Teacher"), "where are you staying?"
>
> "Come," he replied, "and you will see."
>
> So they went and saw where he was staying, and they spent that day with him. It was about four in the afternoon.
>
> Andrew, Simon Peter's brother, was one of the two who heard what John had said and who had

followed Jesus. The first thing Andrew did was to find his brother Simon and tell him, "We have found the Messiah" (that is, the Christ). And he brought him to Jesus.

Jesus looked at him and said, "You are Simon, son of John. You will be called Cephas" (which, when translated, is Peter). (John 1:35–42)

In a second call, Peter, Andrew, John, and James were doing their work as fishermen. Jesus asked them to follow him, and they immediately left their nets and followed him.

As Jesus was walking beside the Sea of Galilee, he saw two brothers, Simon called Peter and his brother Andrew. They were casting a net into the lake, for they were fishermen. "Come, follow me," Jesus said, "and I will send you out to fish for people." At once they left their nets and followed him.

Going on from there, he saw two other brothers, James son of Zebedee and his brother John. They were in a boat with their father Zebedee, preparing their nets. Jesus called them, and immediately they left the boat and their father and followed him. (Matthew 4:18–22)

They went with Jesus as he was "teaching in synagogues, preaching the good news of the kingdom, and healing every disease and sickness among the people" (Matthew 4:23). Later on, they returned to their fishing business.

The third time they were called, they stayed with him permanently. They were washing their nets, after a mostly unproductive day of fishing, when Jesus told them, "Put out into deep water, and let down the nets for a catch" (Luke 5:4). They did, and they caught such a large catch of fish that their nets began to break and the boats began to sink. Peter and the others were astonished at the catch. "Then Jesus said to Simon, 'Don't be afraid; from now on you will catch men.' So they pulled their boats up on shore, left everything and followed him" (Luke 5:10). This time, Jesus helped the disciples when they had a personal need, and that made a big difference in how committed they became to him and to following God's plan.

> One day as Jesus was standing by the Lake of Gennesaret, the people were crowding around him and listening to the word of God. He saw at the water's edge two boats, left there by the fishermen, who were washing their nets. He got into one of the boats, the one belonging to Simon, and asked him to put out a little from shore. Then he sat down and taught the people from the boat.
>
> When he had finished speaking, he said to Simon, "Put out into deep water, and let down the nets for a catch."
>
> Simon answered, "Master, we've worked hard all night and haven't caught anything. But because you say so, I will let down the nets."
>
> When they had done so, they caught such a large number of fish that their nets began to break. So they signaled their partners in the other boat to come and help them, and they came and filled both boats so full that they began to sink.
>
> When Simon Peter saw this, he fell at Jesus' knees and said, "Go away from me, Lord; I am a sinful man!"

For he and all his companions were astonished at the catch of fish they had taken, and so were James and John, the sons of Zebedee, Simon's partners.

Then Jesus said to Simon, "Don't be afraid; from now on you will fish for people." So they pulled their boats up on shore, left everything and followed him. (Luke 5:1–11)

People have various reactions to the calling. One reaction is that they reject it for lack of understanding. Another reaction is that they accept it with joy, but because they do not get grounded in the basics of God's plan, they fall away when trouble or persecution comes. Another reaction is that they accept it, but they allow their own plans to lead them into not following God's plan, and they become unfruitful. The reaction that pleases God and leads to eternal life, however, is when the unbeliever hears the Gospel, accepts Jesus as his or her Savior and Lord, joins a Bible study group and church, and gets discipled to the point that he or she begins to share God's plan with others and disciples them so there is a multiplication of effort and results (Matthew 13:3–8, 19–23).

Discussion Questions

1. What reactions to the Gospel lead to unfruitfulness?

2. What reactions to the Gospel lead to fruitfulness?

3. What does it mean to produce a crop, yielding one hundred, sixty, or thirty times what was sown?

REPRODUCTION—APPOINTMENT

Hundreds of people followed Jesus from place to place. From this large group, Jesus appointed twelve disciples to the positions of apostles. Jesus chose them to be his inner circle and to receive a more intense training, spending more time closely with him (Mark 3:13–19).

Before making his appointments, Jesus spent a night praying to God. This task of making the appointments was very important because it would be from the twelve apostles that Jesus would begin his Church (Luke 6:12–16). The apostles were there when the Holy Spirit came at Pentecost, baptizing them in the Holy Spirit and with power so they could grow the early church.

The apostles were a group of ordinary men with diverse backgrounds. The one personality trait that they had, which was very important to following Jesus, was obedience.

Today, Bible study leaders should have regular meetings in which they teach God's plan to their members and take them out on evangelistic missions so they can learn by example what a believer should do.

Discussion Question

1. What was the most important personality trait that the apostles shared?

REPRODUCTION—DELEGATION

Jesus delegated or sent out the twelve apostles with the responsibility of sharing the Gospel and with the authority and power to drive out evil spirits and to heal every disease and sickness. Their message was that the kingdom of heaven is near. They were sent out, two by two, for six teams of two. Jesus could have sent each one out by himself and covered more ground, but then, the apostles would not have had the fellowship they needed to support each other, especially in adverse situations.

Jesus sent them out with a principle to guide them: "Freely you have received, freely give" (Matthew 10:8). Since God has been so generous with his believers, they should be generous with others. Another principle that Jesus gave them was that if you meet people who are not open to your message, move on to another person. Jesus said, "If anyone will not welcome you or listen to your words, shake the dust off your feet when you leave that home or town" (Matthew 10:14). Remember the adage, some will, some won't, next.

Tough situations were bound to occur, and Jesus gave the apostles this admonition: "I am sending you out like sheep among wolves. Therefore, be as shrewd as snakes and as innocent as doves" (Matthew 10:16).

Jesus also sent out seventy-two others with the message that "the kingdom of God is near you." They were sent out ahead of Jesus to every town and place where he was about to go. Jesus wanted to reach as many people as possible because a lot of people had not heard the Gospel yet. Jesus gave the same admonition to the seventy-two that he had given to the twelve: "I am sending you out like lambs among wolves" (Luke 10:3).

Discussion Questions

1. What does it mean to be called, appointed, and delegated?

2. What does it mean to be sent out like "lambs among wolves"?

REPRODUCTION—ACCOUNTABILITY

⟋

"When the twelve apostles returned, they reported to Jesus all that they had done. With joy they reported their successes and victories" (Luke 9:10).

When the seventy-two returned, they reported to Jesus their victories over Satan and his demons. And Jesus rejoiced with them (Luke 10:17–20).

Today, the disciples who are sent out two by two should return to report to the group how the Holy Spirit helped them achieve victories and also share some of the challenges they faced. Accountability is good for answering questions about productivity too. New ideas can be shared and discussed to generate synergy for more opportunities to reach the field of unbelievers who are ready to believe and become fruitful for God.

Discussion Questions

1. Who was defeated by the seventy-two?

2. At whom should disciples aim their attacks when trying to win spiritual battles?

REPRODUCTION—INCREASE

The more sowers and reapers there are, the greater the chance of increase in the growth of the Church. God is in control of the cutting back and pruning to increase the fruitfulness of the disciples. Jesus said, "The kingdom of heaven has been forcefully advancing, and forceful men lay hold of it" (Matthew 11:12). When sowers and reapers follow God's plan and persevere in their work, increase will happen.

> I am the true vine, and my Father is the gardener. He cuts off every branch in me that bears no fruit, while every branch that does bear fruit he prunes so that it will be even more fruitful. You are already clean because of the word I have spoken to you. Remain in me, as I also remain in you. No branch can bear fruit by itself; it must remain in the vine. Neither can you bear fruit unless you remain in me. (John 15:1–4)

Jesus gave the parable of the mustard seed and the yeast to show how the church, from its small beginnings, would grow into a worldwide organization and movement.

> Then Jesus asked, "What is the kingdom of God like? What shall I compare it to? It is like a mustard seed, which a man took and planted in his garden. It grew and became a tree, and the birds perched in its branches."
>
> Again he asked, "What shall I compare the kingdom of God to? It is like yeast that a woman took

and mixed into about sixty pounds of flour until it worked all through the dough." (Luke 13:18–21)

Today, using God's plan for sharing the Gospel, increase through reproduction is expected. Disciples are called, appointed, delegated, held accountable for productivity, and when new disciples are added these new disciples go through the same reproduction process. This reproduction process repeats itself, over and over again, causing multiplication.

Discussion Question

1. How will increase through multiplication occur in the Church?

Gospel Presentation

What Everyone Wants

- After death, everyone wants to go to heaven, especially considering the alternative, which is hell.
- Most people do not think too much about their eternal destiny. They are too busy working their own plans and living life.
- Jesus said there is only one way to get to heaven, and that is through putting their faith in him as Savior and Lord and then living according to God's plan.
- But one might ask, why do I have to do that? What's wrong with living according to my plan?

The Problem for Unbelievers

- Each of us has a sin nature, which causes us to sin.
- Unbelievers have a personal record book in which every sin that they have ever committed is recorded.
- On Judgment Day, God looks at these sins and pronounces a guilty verdict.
- All guilty persons get sent to hell for all eternity.

No Problem for Believers

- Believers have a sin nature too, which causes them to sin.
- Believers have a personal record book in which no sins are recorded because their sins have been forgiven.
- On Judgment Day, God does not see any sins and pronounces an innocent verdict.
- All believers get sent to heaven for all eternity.

The Judgment for Unbelievers

- Unbelievers cannot produce good fruit because they do not follow God's plan.
- The angels will gather everyone who does not produce good fruit, and they will be sent to hell.
- Hell is described in unpleasant terms, such as a lake of fire, an unquenchable fire, a place where the worm does not die, and a fiery furnace where there will be weeping and gnashing of teeth.

The Judgment for Believers

- Believers produce good fruit because they are saved and follow God's plan.
- The angels will gather everyone who produces good fruit, and they will be sent to heaven.
- Heaven, in the Gospels, is not described as well as hell, but we do know that it is a place where God, angels, and believers live together in a perfect environment for all eternity. The believers will experience their third step of eternal life or salvation (after justification and sanctification) which is glorification: the reception of their new, perfect, and glorified bodies which will experience no pain or suffering.

Good Works

- Unbelievers believe that they can resolve their sin problem by doing good works.
- They hope they can do enough good works to outweigh their sins and earn a place in heaven, but God's judgment does not work like that.
- All God has to see is one sin in your personal record book, and he will pronounce you guilty and condemn you to hell.

Eternal Life

- Eternal life is by grace through faith, not good works.
- Eternal life is a gift because Jesus did all the work for believers when he died on the cross.
- When a believer experiences eternal life, several things occur: he or she is forgiven, redeemed, born again, and baptized in the Holy Spirit.
- Forgiveness frees people from being found guilty of sins.
- Redemption frees people from being slaves to their sinful natures.
- Being born again provides regenerated spirits in order to live with God.
- The baptism of the Holy Spirit empowers disciples to work God's plan with power.

Forgiveness

- The remedy for sins being recorded in the personal books in heaven is forgiveness.
- Forgiveness occurs because of Jesus's death on the cross.
- All sins are taken from the personal books and laid on Jesus.

- Jesus died to pay the price for sins so that they would be forgiven.
- For those who put their faith in him, their personal books are cleared of all sin.

Redemption

- The remedy for being slaves to sin is redemption.
- The sin nature is the root cause of the problem for committing sins, and it causes people to be slaves to sin.
- Redemption occurs because Jesus died on the cross in the believer's place.
- Jesus's death paid the ransom to purchase believers out of sin, judgment, and eternal punishment in hell.

Born Again

- To be born again is for your spirit to be regenerated.
- Jesus regenerates believers' spirits so that they can see and understand God's plan and experience a vital relationship with God.

Baptism in the Holy Spirit

- Jesus is the one who baptizes in the Holy Spirit.
- Jesus said that the baptism in the Holy Spirit would give believers the power needed to work God's plan effectively.

Repentance

- Repentance is turning from working your own plan to working God's plan.

- For unbelievers, working their own plan means working any plan but God's plan, which usually has to do with some self-interest: career, money, hobbies, good works, etc.
- Jesus's first disciples left their businesses to follow him. They believed that he was the Messiah and were willing to repent of their own plans to learn God's plan, as taught by Jesus.
- These were hardworking men who heard Jesus talk about eternal life in heaven and the need to repent and believe the good news, and they decided that was what they wanted. They believed that Jesus knew the plan to get there.

Faith

- Eternal life is by grace through faith in Jesus.
- The Gospel message is that Jesus is the Messiah who died on the cross in everyone's place to deliver unbelievers from sin and hell so they could have eternal life with God.
- Unbelievers can express their faith in Jesus through prayer. A prayer of faith in Jesus can be as simple as:
- Heavenly Father, I believe that your Son, Jesus, is the Messiah who died on the cross in my place so that I may have eternal life with you. I accept your free gift and give my life to you to teach me how to live life according to your plan. Amen.

Discipleship

- After accepting Jesus as your Savior and Lord, it is very important to obtain a Bible, join a Bible study group, and attend a church. A Bible study group and church will help you get to know God's plan and to live it.

Printed in the United States
by Baker & Taylor Publisher Services